FAMOUS ★ FACES

BRITISH MUSIC

Matt Anniss

D1313321

Badger LEARNING

Badger Publishing Limited
Oldmeadow Road,
Hardwick Industrial Estate,
King's Lynn PE30 4JJ
Telephone: 01438 791 037

www.badgerlearning.co.uk

2 4 6 8 10 9 7 5 3 1

British Musicians ISBN 978-1-78464-367-6

Publisher: Susan Ross
Project editor: Paul Rockett
Senior editor: Danny Pearson
Editorial coordinator: Claire Morgan
Designer: Jason Billin / BDS Publishing Ltd

Picture credits: Agencja Fotograficzna Caro/Alamy: 5; Christian Bertrand/Dreamstime.com:
29; Christian Bertrand/Shuttertock: 30; Marc D Birnbach/Shutterstock: 22; DFree/Shutterstock:
8; Dwphotos/Dreamstime.com: 4, 25; Featureflash/Shutterstock: 9, 10, 18; hurricanehank/
Shutterstock: 28; JStone/Shutterstock: 1, 14, 17; Paul Keeling/Shutterstock: 16; New York Daily
News Archive/gettyimages: 11; Luigi Orru/Alamy: 23; Andrea Raffin/Shutterstock: cover, 6;
Mark Sepple/Dreamstime.com: 19; Tinseltown/Shutterstock: 13, 26; WENN Ltd/Alamy: 12;
yakub88/Shutterstock: 20; ZUMA Press, Inc/Alamy: 24.

Attempts to contact all copyright holders have been made. If any omitted would care to
contact Badger Learning, we will be happy to make appropriate arrangements.

FAMOUS ★ FACES

Contents

Vocabulary

Do you know these words?
Look them up in a dictionary and then see how they
are used in the book.

conquer   pioneer

grime   promoting

LED   sensations

officially   statistics

CHAPTER 1

GLOBAL SUPERSTARS

British musicians are among the most popular on the planet. From America to Australia, music fans can't get enough of British singers, bands and producers.

In 2013, one in every eight albums bought around the world was by a British act – that's 13% of all global music sales. According to statistics, sales of British music topped £1 billion in 2014.

Today, Britain is home to some of the most popular and recognisable musicians on the planet.

Singer-songwriter Ed Sheeran worked hard to get to the top. As a teenager, he played hundreds of shows a year for little or no money, and even spent time sleeping rough in London to pursue his dream.

His big break came in 2010 after he bought a one-way plane ticket to Los Angeles. While there, he met R&B star Jamie Foxx, who offered the British youngster time in his studio.

Today, Sheeran is one of the world's most successful musicians. His second album, *X*, has sold over six million copies, while his songs have been listened to over two billion times on leading music streaming site Spotify.

★★ FACT FILE:

ED SHEERAN

Date of birth: 17 February 1991

Famous songs: 'Give Me Love'
'Thinking Out Loud'
'Don't'

Fun fact: Has written songs with, and for, One Direction and Taylor Swift.

Following the success of her 2011 album, 21, Adele has become one of the most recognisable British singers in the world. Amazingly, it was the biggest-selling album in the world for two years running, a feat that had never previously been achieved in the history of music!

Some British musicians find it hard to become popular in the USA, but Adele was a hit straight away. Her first album, *19*, was so popular in the USA that she was named Best New Artist at the 2009 Grammy Awards.

★★ FACT! ★★

Adele's 'Someone Like You' is officially the UK's most downloaded song of all time.

LEGENDS
OF BRITISH MUSIC

Cheryl Fernandez-Versini, better known as Cheryl Cole, has hit the top of the UK singles charts more than any other British female singer. As of 2014, she'd had five solo number one hits, as well as four as part of the pop group Girls Aloud.

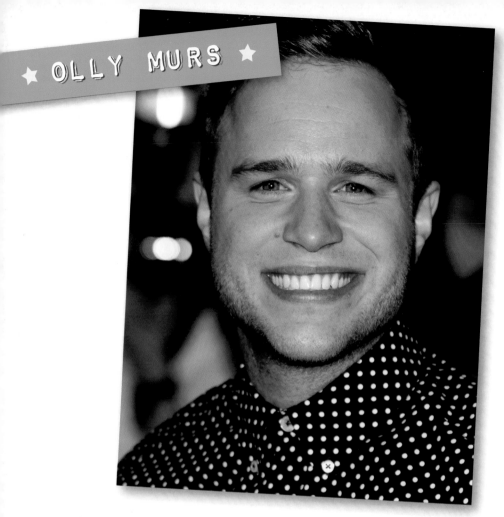

★ OLLY MURS ★

Before rocketing to fame in 2009 as a contestant on the TV talent show *The X Factor*, Olly Murs worked in a call centre. Now, he's so rich that he probably never has to work again!

The Essex-born singer started to become well known in the USA after supporting One Direction on their 2012 concert tour. He's also made appearances on some of the country's most popular TV shows, including *Dancing with the Stars*.

THE DAILY NEWS

BEATLEMANIA SWEEPS THE UNITED STATES

The Beatles were the first British band to 'conquer the USA'. On 9 February 1964, they made their first appearance on American television. 74 million people tuned in to watch, setting off a wave of 'Beatlemania' that would make them the most popular band in history. To date, they've sold an estimated 276 million records!

CHAPTER 2:
NEW HEROES

It can take some British musicians years of hard work to become successful. Others become 'overnight sensations', tasting success at a young age. These are the 'new heroes' who will push British music forwards in the years to come. They're proof that if you're good enough, you're old enough!

While she was at university, Ellie Goulding faced a tough choice: continue her studies or chase her dream of music success. She chose music, and has never looked back.

After being named the 'Sound of 2010' by the BBC, the singer-songwriter has gone on to record huge hits in both the UK and USA. In 2011, she even performed at the Royal Wedding of the Duke and Duchess of Cambridge!

Every successful musician needs a little luck.
For Sam Smith, that came when he met dance band
Disclosure. They asked him to sing on their track
'Latch', which went on to top the UK charts in 2012.

By 2014, Smith was one of the most celebrated British musicians around the world. At the 2015 Grammys, he scooped four awards, including Best New Artist and Song of the Year.

He achieved all of this by the age of 23!

★★ FACT FILE:

SAM SMITH

Date of birth: 19 May 1992

Famous songs: 'Stay With Me',
'I'm Not The Only One',
'Lay Me Down'

Fun fact: When he was 15, Sam's mum was sacked from her job as a banker. The bank thought she was spending too much time promoting his singing career!

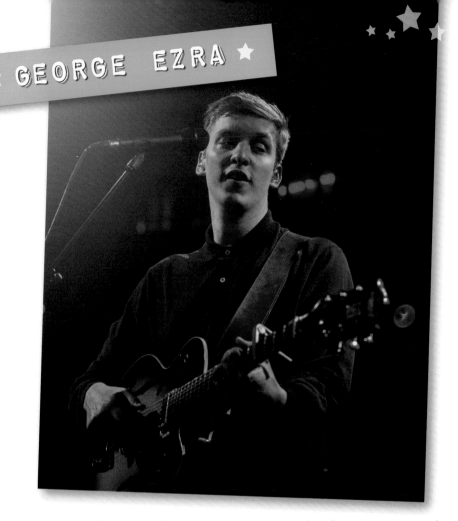

Sam Smith's rapid rise seems positively slow compared to that of fellow singer-songwriter George Ezra. He was studying music at college in Bristol when his big break came, aged just 19.

This was 2013. By the time he celebrated his 20th birthday, he'd already released his first song, 'Budapest'. A year later, it would become one of the biggest selling records of 2014. After Ezra's first album, *Wanted On Voyage*, hit the top of the charts, he headed off to tour the USA with Sam Smith.

LEGEND
OF BRITISH MUSIC

Sam Smith, George Ezra and Ed Sheeran will struggle to sell more records than Sir Elton John, officially the most successful British male singer of all time. Since 1970, he's reportedly sold over 160 million singles, albums and downloads, including 112 million in the USA alone!

★★ FACT! ★★

Elton John's 'Candle in the Wind 1997' sold an amazing 4.9 million copies, making it the most successful song in the history of the British pop charts!

Not all the 'new heroes' of British music are immediately successful. Take Paloma Faith, for example. Before hitting the big time, she worked as a dancer, actress and backing singer for other British musicians, including Amy Winehouse and Basement Jaxx.

It was her second album as a solo singer, 2012's *Fall To Grace*, which rocketed her towards the 'A-list'. It was so popular that many famous songwriters offered to work with her, including Pharrell Williams.

CHAPTER 3

FESTIVAL FAVOURITES

The success of many British bands and singers doesn't come from big chart hits, but rather a reputation for delivering electric live performances. These are the 'festival favourites' – acts who can regularly be found headlining music festivals such as Glastonbury.

Glastonbury Festival, held on a farm in Somerset, has been the biggest music festival in Britain for over 40 years. Legendary British bands that have delivered memorable performances at Glastonbury include:

- ★ Blur
- ★ The Rolling Stones
- ★ Kasabian
- ★ Oasis
- ★ Radiohead

★★ FACT! ★★

The Rolling Stones' A Bigger Bang world tour (2005-2007) was the most successful ever by a British band. They played 144 shows, entertaining an astonishing 4.86 million fans!

It would be fair to say that Coldplay know how to put on a great show. During their Mylo Xyloto world tour (2011-12), they gave every audience member a special, high-tech wristband, known as a Xyloband.

The wristbands contained LED lights, which lit up, flashed and changed colour in time with the songs. The wristbands were a huge hit with fans, and helped Coldplay to win Best Live Act at the 2013 BRIT Awards.

That tour was a huge success for Coldplay. It saw them perform to over two million people, in over 60 cities around the world.

★★ FACT FILE: ★★

COLDPLAY

Year formed: 1996

Famous songs: 'Yellow', 'Viva La Vida', 'Fix You', 'Clocks'

Fun fact: As part of their 2012 world tour, Coldplay performed at the closing ceremony of the London Paralympics.

★ MUMFORD & SONS ★

While most bands love performing at music festivals, very few run their own big events. However, that's exactly what popular folk-rock band Mumford & Sons do.

Since 2012, Mumford & Sons have hosted regular, weekend-long 'mini-festivals', known as Gentlemen of the Road Stopovers. These feature performances from the band, plus some of their favourite musicians.

In 2015, Mumford & Sons ran 'Stopover' events in the USA and Aviemore, Scotland.

Indie-rockers alt-J are almost certainly one of the most in-demand bands on the global festival circuit. Known for their thrilling performances and heavy sound, the four-piece spend each summer flying between events all around the world.

In 2015 alone, the Leeds-based band performed at festivals as far afield as India, Canada, Lebanon, Germany, Norway and the USA. They still found time to squeeze in an appearance at Glastonbury, too!

THE DAILY NEWS

ARCTIC MONKEYS
TAKE LONDON BY STORM!

On 27 July 2012, Arctic Monkeys wowed the opening ceremony of the London 2012 Olympic Games with an electric performance.

The indie-rock band played two songs to a packed Olympic Stadium, and hundreds of millions of people watching on television around the world.

It was a memorable moment for a band that had previously headlined the Glastonbury Festival. Ten years earlier, they were playing to tiny audiences in their home city of Sheffield, South Yorkshire.

Britain is home to some of the world's most popular rappers, dance music producers, and DJs. These are people who create and play music designed to make people dance and have a good time.

Today's 'electronic aces' are just the latest in a long line of dance stars from Britain. Legends of British dance music include:

★ Fatboy Slim
★ Basement Jaxx
★ The Chemical Brothers
★ The Prodigy

★★ FACT! ★★

Britain's biggest selling song of 2014 was 'Happy' by American singer Pharrell Williams. The biggest hit by a British act was 'Rather Be' by the electronic dance group Clean Bandit.

Calvin Harris is now one of the richest dance musicians on the planet. It wasn't so long ago that he was recording music in his bedroom, using an old computer.

It took a while for Harris to become a success. In 2006, after years of struggle, he decided to post some of his songs on the internet. That led to a recording contract with a big record company, and he's never looked back.

Today, he earns huge sums of money DJing around the world. He's also an in-demand producer, and has worked with big stars such as Rihanna, Example and Tinchy Stryder.

★★ FACT FILE: ★★

CALVIN HARRIS

Date of birth: 17 January 1984

Famous songs: 'Summer', 'Feels So Close', 'Bounce'

Fun fact: According to Forbes magazine, Harris earned an astonishing £42.8 million in 2014, making him the world's richest DJ.

★ JESSIE WARE ★

Jessie Ware is now best known for making pop songs, but it was dance music that earned her a shot at the big time. In 2010, she was featured on a popular underground club hit by SBTRKT, and a star was born.

Her successful 2014 album, *Tough Love*, was made with the assistance of an all-star cast, including top DJ Julio Bashmore and fellow British singer Ed Sheeran.

★ DISCLOSURE ★

British dance music is no stranger to successful brothers, with Orbital's Paul and Phil Hartnoll becoming festival favourites in the 1990s. Guy and Howard Lawrence, the brothers behind Disclosure, have been even more successful.

Now one of the biggest electronic acts on the planet, Disclosure hit the big time when their songs 'Latch' and 'White Noise' sold an amazing 600,000 copies.

Rapper Dizzee Rascal is a pioneer. During the 2000s, he helped develop a new style of dance music known as 'grime'.

In 2003, he became the youngest musician to win the Mercury Music Prize. Nine years later, he played a starring role at the opening ceremony of the London 2012 Olympics, which took place close to where he grew up in East London.

What was the name of the wristbands given to Coldplay fans during the band's 2011-2012 world tour? (page 20)

★ ★ ★ ★ ★ ★

How many awards did Sam Smith win at the 2015 Grammys? (page 15)

★ ★ ★ ★ ★ ★

Which British musician performed at the Royal Wedding of the Duke and Duchess of Cambridge? (page 13)

★ ★ ★ ★ ★ ★

Which British musician topped the worldwide album charts for two years running? (page 8)

★ ★ ★ ★ ★ ★

Who is the most successful British male singer of all time? (page 17)

★ ★ ★ ★ ★ ★

Which two British acts, featured in this book, performed at the London 2012 Olympics? (pages 24 and 30)

★ ★ ★ ★ ★ ★

★ INDEX ★